LET'S GET REAL

Let's Get Real

FOR SPIRITUAL GROWTH AND STABILITY

By

Sarah Newkirk Pearson

LET'S GET REAL

Let's Get Real
Copyright © 2016
Sarah N. Pearson

ALL RIGHTS RESERVED
No portion of this publication may be reproduced, stored in any electronic system, or transmitted in any form or by any means, electronic, mechanical, photocopy, recording or otherwise without the expressed written consent of the author. Brief quotations may be used in literary reviews.

ISBN: 978-0-9970-227-3-5

Taylor House Publishing
P.O. Box 720
Virginia Beach, VA 23451
(757) 214-4926
taylorpublishinghouse@gmail.com

For more information contact:

Sarah N. Pearson
pearsonsarah@att.net

Printed in the USA
Precision Printing
1300 Priority Lane
Chesapeake, VA 23324

Dedication

This book is dedicated to my children: Aletta, her husband Rodger; Jerome, his wife Joyal; Benita and Keith.

A special memory to my mother, Mary Wilson Newkirk

Thanks to all my family and friends who brought silk flowers at my 75th birthday party to make the beautiful bouquet represented on the cover in my favorite color -- pink.

LET'S GET REAL

ABOUT THE AUTHOR

Sarah Pearson, a retired nurse, resides in Goldsboro, North Carolina. She was married to Johnnie Pearson for 22 years, until he went home to be with the Lord in April, 2011.

As a young girl, she joined Antioch Baptist Church and gave her life to Jesus. After a period of "straying," she rededicated her life with an iron intent on service to the Kingdom of God and her church. At Antioch, she sang with the Mass Choir and was president of the Mother/Deaconess Board.

Her benevolent ministries included starting an outreach to the private homes of the sick and shut-in, nursing homes and hospitals, whereby soup was delivered and prayer and Bible Study conducted. For ten years, she and Deacon Pearson led the noonday prayer. Sarah became a diligent student of the Bible, a Sunday School Teacher, and wrote for the local gospel newspaper, "The Good News Gazette." In 2004 she accepted the call to teach the gospel and was ordained a Minister.

In 2005 she began to serve at the Philadelphia Community Church under the leadership of her children – Pastors Rodger and Aletta Taylor. At "PCC" she has continued to serve with joy! Her past and present commitments include the Praise Team, Singles Ministry, Sunday School Teacher, Head of Mother/Deaconess Ministry, and Head of Benevolence. Since uniting with PCC she has been elevated to the office of Elder and executes her position well. Elder Pearson has a genuine concern for others and reaches out to anyone in need.

Psalm 27 is her favorite scripture for it has "brought her through many attacks of the enemy and helped her maintain a firm foundation in Christ." Her purpose in the kingdom is to be an example, a living sacrifice. Elder Pearson is an anointed Prayer Warrior. She has four children, 13 grand-children and seven great-grandchildren.

LET'S GET REAL

TABLE OF CONTENTS

A LIVING SACRIFICE ------------------------------9
AN UNFORGIVING SPIRIT------------------------11
ANGER ---13
BACKSLIDDEN HEART --------------------------16
BEATITUDES --------------------------------------- 19
COUNT THE COST-------------------------------- 21
DELIGHT YOURSELVES IN THE LORD ----- 25
ESTABLISHED IN THE WORD OF GOD ------ 28
EXTRAORDINARY CHRISTIAN (PERSON)---31
FAITHFUL SERVANT -----------------------------34
GOD'S KINGDOM --------------------------------- 38
GOSSIP -- 40
HOLINESS -- 43
HYPOCRISY --47
JEALOUSY -- 49
LEADERSHIP -------------------------------------- 52
LIGHT OF THE WORLD --------------------------56
LOVE THY NEIGHBOR -------------------------- 59
PEACE --- 62
RESURRECTION ---------------------------------- 65

LET'S GET REAL

RUTH AND NAOMI	67
SELFLESS LOVE VS LIKE	70
SPIRIT OF FEAR	73
SPIRIT OF HUMILITY	77
SPIRIT OF TRUTH	80
STUBBORNNESS—REBELLION	83
SUFFERING	86
THE JOY OF GIVING	90
THE LORD IS MY SHEPHERD	93
UNIQUE	96
UNITY	98
UNITY OF BELIEVERS	101
WHO DO YOU SERVE AND WHY	105
WORRY	108
YOU CAN MAKE IT	112

LET'S GET REAL

A LIVING SACRIFICE

Another word for sacrifice is "surrender." Romans chapter 12 verse 1 tells us to present our bodies a living sacrifice, holy and acceptable unto God which is our reasonable service. It is one thing to be saved but another to be surrendered. Man was created by and for God to be mastered by Him not for us to be our own master. When one surrenders, he/she is ready for anything--service or sacrifice. Are you ready for anything? Well, I'm still striving in that area among others; striving to give God everything happily and wholeheartedly.

As Christ was raised from the dead with all power in His hands giving us the victory, sin and death have no more rule over us. Our old natures are crucified, the body of sin is destroyed and we are to be servers of sin no more. Neither are our members to be used as instruments of unrighteousness. What are our members? They are our eyes, ears, feet, hands, our whole mortal bodies. The Bible tells us to be holy as the Father in heaven is holy; and if he says we are able, we can walk in the light as he is in the light. Walking in the scripture means the life we live. Our attitudes and mannerisms change toward ourselves, sin, others, and most of all towards Jesus Christ. We delight ourselves in the Lord and the things pertaining to Him. We talk, think and act differently. He has put a distinct quality in all of us for His purpose and only for Him. Remember, the happiest people are not those who have everything, but those who make the best of what they have.

In closing, ask yourself these questions—1.) How many have I served? 2.) How much have I given? 3.) What have I done for my Lord and Savior? Christ came to minister, not to be ministered unto. So let's get real!

AN UNFORGIVING SPIRIT

Forgiving has nothing to do with feeling like it, wanting to or not. It is an order from God, just as love is not an option. If we expect to be forgiven by our heavenly Father, we must forgive one another (Matthew 6:15). Unforgiveness is the source of many mental, emotional, and physical disturbances. We certainly cannot grow spiritually with an unforgiving heart. It can cause depression, bitterness and malice, leading to hatred if not uprooted. The Bible tells us to forgive and continue walking in love. Sometimes this is accomplished only through lots of prayer and submitting to God. There are times we are our worst enemy, yet we spend much time fighting the supposed enemy without.

The unforgiving attitude is a good example of a rebellious, disobedient, unsurrendered soul. It leaves way for evil spirits to enter. Think about it next time you sing the song "I Surrender All." Sometimes it seems much easier to forgive someone who we know little or nothing about than those we know well. God told us vengeance is His and He will fight the battle. I know He will from experience. Read the parable of the result of the unforgiving servant in Matthew 18:23-35. Remember, we reap what we sow, so let's get real!

ANGER

What is anger? Anger is a strong feeling of displeasure. The Bible tells us to get angry but sin not. How many of us can get angry, and think no evil, speak no evil, or do no evil? That's just a question to think about. Are you aware that whomever you allow to anger you has control over you? However God is to be the Controller of our lives, not man or the things of this world. So be quick to hear God's word, slow to speak and slow to wrath (violent anger or rage). Let not the sun go down upon your wrath. Get it right with whomever it concerns before you sleep at night.

Anger is a sign of power seeking, self-seeking, fear, control, jealousy, bitterness and malice. When we put off the old man and put on the new, those things are put away along with other un-Christ-like characteristics. John 14:1 tell us "Let not your heart be troubled; ye believe in God, believe also in me." Why should we worry? We have taken it out of God's hand when we worry about anything.

Anger causes destruction, violent behavior,

and hatred and vengeance towards what or who should be admired. Did you know that stubbornness derives from anger and is a type of idolatry? Saints, put on the whole armor of God so you will be able to stand against the wiles of Satan.

Uncontrollable anger is one of his most powerful strongholds, especially in the body of Christ. It destroys relationships. Have you heard of the pray-away plan? When the angry spirit begins to rise within, begin to pray. See which prevails. Obedience and prayer are the answers. The scripture tells us to cast all, not some, but all our cares upon Jesus for He cares for us.

Also the word says come unto Him all ye that labor and are heavy laden and He will give you rest from whatever troubles you may have. We must believe! James 3:18 tells us that the fruit of righteousness is sown in peace of them that make peace. Vengeance is mine says the Lord, I will repay (Romans 12:19). Matthew 5:22 says that "whosoever is angry with his brother without a cause is in danger of the judgement."

LET'S GET REAL

How do you deal with an angry man? Well, a soft answer turns away wrath, but grievous words stir up anger. Yes, Jesus became angry and went into the temple and cast out them who bought and sold, saying to them "My house is a house of prayer" (Mark 11:5 and Luke 19:45/46). He is a God of mercy, also a God of wrath; however He controls His anger, it doesn't control Him.

One main reason the body of Christ lacks power is anger prevails over agape love. I say to you, especially saints of Christ, be happy in Jesus even when things seem to be going wrong and grieve not the Holy Spirit. Put away evil speaking and anger for God blesses us according to our obedience and faith; seek peace and pursue it, especially those of the household of faith. Wherever you may be--at home, on the job, in the streets or at play… LET'S BE REAL!

BACKSLIDDEN HEART

Backsliding is 1) turning away from the gospel (Gal. 3: 1-5), 2) leaving your first love (Rev. 2:4) or 3) turning back to the world (II Tim. 4:10).

It is prompted by several things, one being a haughty spirit. Proverbs 16:18 states "pride goes before destruction, and a haughty spirit before a fall." A humble spirit is the way. Many are lifted up in heart when they prosper (Deut. 8:12-14), especially materialistically. Then, they forget from whence they came and who brought them where they are.

Tribulation causes backsliding when circumstances come in our lives to prove us (Matt. 13:21). We give up very quickly if we are not rooted in the Lord. When persecution arises because of the word, we get offended because of what people say or think. Christ said "in this world we will have tribulation; but be of good cheer. I have overcome the world."

Spiritual blindness is a precursor to backsliding as well (II Peter 1: 5-9). Many backslide when they withdraw from total surrender to God and give in to self-pleasing spirits. We may have backslidden in heart, but still be religious from the outer appearance (spiritual show). Other signs of backsliding are lack of spiritual enjoyment, loss of interest in truly spiritual conversation, and missing scheduled services; especially prayer meetings.

If we don't truly enjoy service to God, we don't truly serve him. Out of the abundance of the heart, the mouth speaks. It should be a joy to talk about Christ and live Christian experiences. If the first love of a Christian continues, he/she will be surely drawn by the Holy Spirit to much prayer.

A backslidden heart shall be filled with its own ways (Prov. 14:24). The backslider's mistakes will be their own because they're not walking with God. His own words, having no control of his tongue, will be full of deadly poison (James 3:8) and in his own cares, he has returned to selfishness. Let's keep in mind that we are new creatures in Christ and old things are put away and all things are new. We must mortify the deeds of the flesh, not suppress them.

How do we recover? Return to your first love and do your first works over again truly from the heart (Rev. 2:5). Despite wandering away from God, He still loves you; for he is an everlasting, loving, and forgiving God. Be faithful and allow nothing or no one to rob you of your reward that is due for diligently serving God. Remember, the joy of the Lord is your strength. Let's Get Real!

LET'S GET REAL

BEATITUDES (SERMON ON THE MOUNT) MATTHEW 5: 1-12

The blessed (happy, fortunate) characteristics of Christ's followers; received only through divine favor, manifested in those who really realize they need God and have complete faith and trust in Him.

Blessed are the poor in spirit: Those who recognize their own poverty of inner spirit and don't have the ability to live a life pleasing to God (Romans 3:9-12). They seek divine assistance to meet this need. They will receive the kingdom of heaven for their trust in Christ (Matthew 5:3).

Blessed are they that mourn: Those who have suffered loss, spiritual or material, in this life.

Blessed are the meek: Those who are genuinely humble, without arrogance and realize all that we have is a gift from God. The greatest example of this is Jesus Christ.

Blessed are they that hunger and thirst for righteousness: Spiritual appetite for the righteousness of God. To live a life that reflects the standards of God. They shall be filled.

Blessed are the merciful: Those who extend kindness, compassion and forgiveness to all needy people without partiality must be aware of the fact and stand before God as spiritually needy people.

Blessed are the pure in heart: Divine cleansing from sin that they might be inwardly clean. They will see God.

Blessed are the peacemakers: The sons (children) of God will inherit the spiritual blessings of God as his children.

Blessed are those who are persecuted: As poor in spirit, they will inherit the kingdom. They are divinely blessed even when they are falsely accused of all manner of evil only because they follow Jesus Christ in the midst of it. Rejoice and be glad because it brings reward. Let's get real!

COUNT THE COST

Count means (1) consider (2) number. Cost means (1) expense (2) suffering. When we accept Jesus Christ as our Lord and Savior, there are responsibilities also accepted. When we buy a home, car, furniture or even consider marriage, we should count the cost. The consequences of our actions are either good or bad, depending on whether we have counted the cost. Paul said in Philippians 3:7, "what things were gain to me I counted loss for Christ." Nothing he had, compared to following Christ.

Jesus was teaching the disciples that He was the bread of life and they must eat of his flesh and drink of His blood or they would have no life in them. However, if they did, they would have eternal life in them. Many of the disciples walked away and said this is a hard saying, who can hear it; and followed him no more (John 6:33-66). Perhaps they didn't understand it, however, Jesus being all-knowing, knew those who would not retreat.

Spiritual meat refers to every word that

comes from the mouth of God. Some may have been told when you accept Jesus Christ, all problems are over and everything will go smoothly. Well, I'm here to tell you, "Not so!" But we do have someone who is our ever present helper, who helps to endure with perseverance (until the end). When it's all over, there's a blessing because He goes through it with us.

Jesus said, "If any man come to me and hate not his father, mother, wife, children, brethren, sister, and also his own life, he cannot be my disciple. Whosoever does not bear his cross and come after me, cannot be my disciple" (Luke 14: 26/27). Cross means redemptive suffering; He's not saying to forsake or neglect your families, especially those of your own household. If any provide not for his own house, he has denied the faith and is worse than an infidel (heathen, unbeliever, or untrustworthy) (I Timothy 5:8).

When your affections are set on anyone or anything more than Christ, then He is second but He needs to be first. Count the cost! When I was younger, I used to hear how Jesus had nowhere to lay his head (Luke 9:58) and thought that meant He was poor. Thank God I finally learned better. It meant He had no ties here on earth; no home, cars, family ties, soul ties or rare treasure. He is the treasure. He didn't come here to stay but to do the works of the Father, as we should be doing.

We must be willing to cast away self, so that our ways will be in harmony with His will. Jesus is enough. Many church members backslide sometimes because they haven't been told about counting the cost. Some have home ties, family ties, job ties, friend ties and other ties that keep them from following Christ. No man having put his hand to the plow and looking back is fit for the kingdom of God. Remember Lot's wife as a reminder of disobedience in looking back?

Christ suffered, was rejected, talked about, lied on and despised although he was blameless and harmless. We can expect the same. When the going gets tough, remember that trials come to strengthen or draw you closer to God.

There is much to be said on counting the cost.

Read Luke 14:25-35. When one considers fornication, adultery, evil speaking of his neighbor, lying, cheating, stealing, and many other sins, first count the cost. Worldly possessions must sometimes be given up. Everything and everyone must go for Jesus. However, he must not be given up for anybody or anyone. In spite of all the persecution, there is still joy, peace, and happiness in following Jesus Christ. He has also made some awesome promises to us for being obedient. So count the cost, and let's get real!

LET'S GET REAL

DELIGHT YOURSELVES IN THE LORD

DELIGHT: Great pleasure in something or someone.

I was glad when they said unto me let us go into the house of the Lord. There should be joy and not drudgery when we enter into God's house (Psalms 122:1). If we expect to receive the desires of our hearts, we must first delight in the Lord (Psalms 37:4). It should be a joy to come before His presence in prayer; not just because it is our duty. To worship and praise Him for what He has already done and for what He will or is going to do.

We must consider our ways; our will must be transformed to His will and ways. Be willing to allow God to change whatever needs changing. Only God and you know what truly needs to be changed in your heart. When we delight in the Lord, we fret not, nor do we covet, because knowing the Lord is faithful and all-wise, He will keep his promise. We don't have to worry. Just trust Him and rest in Him and put all things in His hand.

Then, we can live every day with peace and confidence. David recognized total dependence on God (I Chron. 29:11/12). In I Kings 3:19, we see Solomon doing the same and so should we; especially our leaders who should joyfully depend on God. When we delight in the Lord, we wait patiently, still serving him with joy, not complaining, with contentment realizing we cannot force Him. We cannot hurry Him or get ahead of Him. His time is perfect.

Many times we try to manipulate our circumstances but that only brings pain, disappointment and sometimes loss. Delight in God's word and know his will. Some say they love the Lord, but have no interest in His word. He is the word (John 1:1).

When we delight in the Lord, we are new creatures; talking, thinking and acting different. When committed to Christ, it is not so easy to give in to temptation, for God is stronger than the strongest. Yokes are destroyed!

When we delight in the Lord, we also delight in the things of God: prayer, church school, Bible study and Sunday worship and praise services. Most of all, we will be controlled by the love of God, which is a virtue that He puts in us. We will have faith, for faith works love and we cannot please him without it.

When the family is falling apart, children not doing right, burdens seem more than you can bear, or whatever the circumstances, abide in the power of God's word without compromising. Abide in Him, for blessed is the man that fears the Lord and delights greatly in His commandments (Psalms 112:1).

Again I say delight yourselves in the Lord and He will give you the desires of your heart (sometimes even more). I'm a witness! So let's get real!

ESTABLISHED IN THE WORD OF GOD

Establish–a permanent condition somewhat like a habit. Just do it without thinking about it. It becomes a part of you. Through wisdom is a house built and by understanding it is established (Proverbs 24:3). When we are established in the word of God and have right understanding of it, the enemy cannot come and take it away with every wind and doctrine.

When you allow understanding to establish your spiritual house it is not about denominational doctrine or traditions of men, but the word of God. When we're established in the word with understanding, we don't have to think about whether or not we're going to church, Bible Study, Sunday school or reading the Bible each day. Wherever you go you will seek these things because you're established in the things of God.

Christ came to give life more abundant and Satan comes to steal it from you. The word is life and if the enemy can steal the word from you before you are established in it, he has your life. You must be established for the word to be a permanent part of you. Your mind must be renewed in the spiritual aspect. The word is pure (Psalms 19:8) and restraining (Psalms 119:11).

Many will end up on the broad and wide road because they don't like restrictions. Thy word have I hid in my heart that I might not sin against thee (Psalms 119:11). Some Christians act like the world because they aren't established in the word. When the word is a permanent part of us we can stop attacks of Satan and keep him from operating in our lives.

The word is our health, wealth, strength and weapon. It is a Christian's livelihood. Establish your hearts in the word of God with the right understanding and be blessed. In all of our getting, we must get an understanding (Proverbs 4:7).

Let me say this… Two ways the enemy can keep us from being established in the word: (1) not spending time in the world daily and (2) keeping us out of the church where the word is taught or preached. Remember, those who hear and doeth the word are like the house built on the rock, a sure foundation, that can't be shaken (Matt. 7:24, Luke 6:48). That rock is Jesus! He that has an ear to hear, let him hear (Matthew 11:15).

The best Christmas gift we all can have at the beginning of the New Year is to be established in the word, attend Church, Sunday school, bible study and of course to Worship Services to see what God has given the messengers. Read your Bible every day, not only with understanding, but also with a change of heart in mind. May you experience the results of God's blessings in the New Year; even more so than last year. Let's Get Real!

LET'S GET REAL

THE EXTRAORDINARY CHRISTIAN/PERSON

My concept of extraordinary is: notably unusual or exceptional; when one goes exceedingly beyond his/her duty. One who if compelled to go one mile, would go two miles; one who is extraordinary; one who will do justice to others whether it is done to him or not. One who can love his enemy, do good instead of evil and bless those who curse them.

Another example of being extraordinary is one who can be exceedingly joyful when undergoing persecution for Christ's sake or another's sake. Another example of an extraordinary person is one who is not too proud to say "I'm sorry" or "Forgive me." When storms come in our lives let us put on the garment of praise instead of the spirit of heaviness, knowing that the battle is the Lord's and we walk by faith not by sight.

Paul was one of the most extraordinary persons in the Bible before his conversion. He was completely sincere from the heart and steadfast in what he believed. I heard someone say he thought getting up coming to Sunday school is extraordinary. I hear people say lots of times "I'm not a morning person." And it does take an extra boost sometimes. However, if we want to be extraordinary, we must make that extra effort. Success sometimes is accomplished by doing more than necessary.

Solomon is another example of an extraordinary person. His wisdom exceeded all the wisdom of Egypt (I Kings 4:29-30). An extraordinary person realizes the strength and power in unity and acts accordingly; as the locust which has no king but come forth all of them in bands. (Proverbs 30:27).

Another example of an extraordinary Christian is one who allows no arrogance to come out of his/her mouth as Christ did not. Also one who is aware of and careful of how he treats another, knowing God is all knowing and actions are weighed by him. An extraordinary Christian will pray exceedingly that he might perfect that which is lacking in his faith.

LET'S GET REAL

Now we know that the most exceedingly above and beyond extraordinary person is our heavenly Father. His thoughts and ways are perfect; always knowing how, when and where to speak; the only perfect one. He used ordinary people to accomplish extraordinary tasks. I say to the household of faith, let us follow the example of Jesus in striving to be extraordinary Christians.

We're given a choice--we can be ordinary or extraordinary, we can be a first mile or a second mile person. Don't be content with doing just enough, do more than enough. We may fall short and make mistakes sometimes. We are ordinary people who, by the grace of God, can be extraordinary. Remember, loving one another is not a recommendation nor an option, but a commandment from God, so be extraordinary and love unconditionally…and Let's Get Real!

FAITHFUL SERVANT

Who is a faithful servant? One who is committed, trustworthy, truthful, having a spiritual well-being in Christ. Is it possible to have faith and not be faithful? I believe it is. Our main purpose of faith is to please God. Even though we do things to please Him, we may not be persistent in doing them. The Bible says great is thy faithfulness; God rewards faithfulness.

There are many little ways of being faithful that we may think don't matter. Example: have you been in a department store and watched someone step over a garment because they didn't put it there, but you picked it up and put it on the rack? That's a type of faithfulness. Or someone knocked something down and didn't pick it up but you did so without saying anything, a type of faithful servant. One more example we may not think about: Does your husband leave his socks on the floor when he takes them off or your wife leave her hosiery on the floor and you pick them up without saying anything? Or do you have to argue about it? All we do must bring glory to

God no matter how small or unimportant it may seem.

Be a faithful servant of God by serving one another with kindness, respect and love, forbearing (putting up with) and forgiving even when mistreated. Part of growing in holiness and righteousness, is being loving and gracious to the unthankful and to those who have injured you one way or another.

It is so easy to be faithful and trust God when things seem to be going smooth or when doing the easy things. What about the difficult things like loving your enemy and blessing those that curse you? We must be faithful in that area also. What about being faithful when it seems as though no one supports you and rejects or opposes you and your ministry, or what you stand for? Remember Jesus went through more than we will ever experience.

Blessed is the servant who is found working when his Lord returns (Matt. 24:46). Saints, we have a lot of work to do. We all want to hear "Well done! Thou good and faithful servant, thou hast been faithful in a few things, I will make you ruler over many." Jesus is faithful to us in many little ways that will bless us but we are too busy looking for the big things. Little things mean a lot to God and they should to us. He that is faithful in the least, is faithful in much (Luke 16:10).

When I think of faithfulness I always remember the three men with the talents; how two gained because they used what they had and one lost what he had because he didn't use it. The same will happen to us if we are not faithful with what He has given us. Many are unthankful for what they have. Some who are married want to be single, some who are single want to be married. Some want bigger churches, some probably wish they had smaller churches; never satisfied. Well, be faithful with what God has given you. Protect and nurture those members well, that you have and God will give you the desires of your heart.

Now I've given some of the expectations of a faithful servant, so we know that an unfaithful servant is just the opposite. Fear none of those things which thou shalt suffer, be faithful unto death, and I (Christ) will give you a crown of life (Rev. 2:10). Sometimes we seem to get excited about everything except seeking God and His presence. A faithful servant must have his/her heart established in the things of God, especially a prayer life, in order to have a real personal relationship with God. True rewards and recognition come from God. So let's get real!

GOD'S KINDGOM

God's kingdom is His will in our lives on earth now. In order to experience the fullness of God's kingdom, we must get rid of many wrong attitudes such as uncontrollable anger, gossip, bitterness, etc. One main spirit that sends others away is an argumentative spirit. How forcible are right words but what does arguing reprove (Job 6:25). Christ never argued. He was provoked, accused, lied on, and rejected among other things, but never stopped to argue. Let's follow his example.

He said what the Father said to say and did what the Father said to do and carried on His mission. To obtain God's kingdom, we must deal with enemies within before we can deal with enemies without. Matthew 13 states what the kingdom is like. It is God's will for His kingdom to come on earth. Luke 12:34 declares where your heart is, there will your treasure be also. Seek first the kingdom of God and His righteousness and you'll find your treasure; for God is in His kingdom. Your treasure is not in your husband, wife, nor children. God created them also for His purpose.

Jesus came to earth to destroy the devil's kingdom by casting out devils, performing miracles, and doing many divine works. When He left His disciples, He stated, "these works shall you do and greater things shall you do" (John 14:12). Saints, we have a lot of work to do. Work is one way we overcome the strategies of Satan. Jesus took the keys from Satan after leaving the cross, gave them to the church, giving her the ability, power, and authority to fight against the wiles of Satan.

Christ said we are either against Him or for Him. If we are not for Him, we will work to bring others to Him. If we're against Him, we'll send others away with our spirits of jealousy, self-centeredness, unforgiveness and just plain meanness. Jesus intended for us to continue the works He began, to establish His kingdom on earth. May you prosper, be in health, even as your soul prospers, which is also God's will. Let's get real!

GOSSIP

Gossip--idle talk or rumors about others. Why does one gossip? I will try to name just a few reasons why people gossip. If it doesn't apply to you as you read it, don't be offended. People gossip because:

1. It expresses anger, bitterness, hatred and related works that can't be expressed to another's face. It causes discord, one of the things that God hates (Proverbs 6:19). Where envy and strife is there is every evil work (James 3:16). Hatred stirs up strife but love covers up all sins (Proverbs 10:12).

2. Pride encourages gossip. "I know what you don't know." "I have what you don't have." Pride is another thing that God hates. It goes before destruction and a haughty spirit before a fall (Proverbs 16:18).

3. Some feel better when they pull others down to their level.

4. Gossip destroys others, their reputation and possibly the whole person. Amidst gossip that is the

main purpose. Isn't that what Satan came to do–steal, kill, and destroy? I am afraid it is (John 10:10). Seek peace and pursue it.

5. One who gossips stretches the truth because of his/her loose tongue. In addition to wayward tongues, hot tempers cool friendships and sharp words dull respect. The Bible says "Be quick to hear, slow to speak and slow to wrath" (James 1:19). If any man among you seem to be religious and bridle not his tongue, he deceives his own heart; this man's religion is in vain (James 1:26).

6. Gossip reveals the nature of the heart; for out of the heart the mouth speaks (Matthew 12:24) and as a man thinks, so is he (Proverbs 23:7). How can we being good, speak evil things?

If someone criticizes you, think and see if truth is in it. If so, change. If not, ignore it and live so the ignorance of foolish men will be put to silence (I Peter 2:15). Do not seek so much to be consoled as to console (comfort). Don't seek so much to be understood as to understand, to be loved as to love. Let us therefore follow after things which make for peace and things wherewith one may edify another (Romans 14:19).

Remember saints, no weapon formed against us will prosper and greater is He that is in us than he that is in the world. Vengeance is mine says the Lord, I will repay. I'm a witness to that. Also remember the main principal in the kingdom of God–we reap what we sow. And sometimes the harvest is greater…so let's get real!

HOLINESS

Holiness, a very broad subject, means Godliness, sanctification, set apart for a specific purpose, leads to holiness; it involves submissiveness to God. We walk to please Him. The body is the temple of the Holy Ghost and is not to be defiled (I Cor. 3:16), but kept in sanctification and honor (I Thess. 4:4, 7) for God has not called us to uncleanness, but to holiness. We believers are now new creatures, a living sacrifice and sanctuary, holy unto God as our reasonable service, ready to be used anytime and anywhere; when we feel like it and when we don't, especially when we don't.

We are to be holy in all manner of conversation, meaning all aspects of our life. It is written "Be ye holy for I am holy" (I Peter 1:5/6) and if He says we can be, we can be. We should always strive for perfection (maturity in Christ). It doesn't mean we will not err but we will live a life of repentance for our Father is faithful to forgive and restore when we come to him and ask truly from the heart.

Holiness is thinking, speaking and acting right. God promised that He would be our father and we would be His sons and daughters. Therefore remembering this among other promises, we must cleanse ourselves from all filthiness of flesh and spirit, perfecting holiness in the fear of God (II Corinthians 7:1). What are some of the ungodly virtues: adultery, fornication, bitterness, unforgiveness, jealousy, lying, strife, and revelries (as being loose, loud and boisterous). We don't act like the world.

Holiness also involves the way we dress. We don't dress as though we're going to a night club like we used to, ladies. We're daughters of a princess; Sarah, Abraham's wife. The scripture says we're to adorn ourselves in modest apparel and be in self-control (I Tim. 2: 9/10). Many think attire has nothing to do with our love for God, but to some extent it does. There are holy standards for males and females to live by as children of God. Godly women should pay attention to bust lines, hemlines and vents in dresses and skirts. Our members are instruments of righteousness.

Holiness brings forth fruit (John 15:8). Ungodliness causes many sorrows (I Timothy 6:10). Sometimes holiness comes through chastisement that we may be partakers of His holiness. Jesus went back to the Father and sent the Holy Ghost to lead and guide us into all truth; holiness is truth. We are not holy just on church days, but even when we're not being watched. We are the church, walking holy every day. Godliness is profitable unto all things having promise of the life to come and that now is (I Timothy 4:8).

When you go fishing and catch a fish, it must be cleaned before it can be used for food. Jesus said, "I will make you fishers of men" (Matt. 4:19). Now when one accepts Jesus Christ as Lord and Savior, he/she must be purged or cleansed also. No, I'm not judging, but it is a basic Bible principal.

The Bible is a holy book and it is our livelihood. Our minds must be renewed from bad thoughts and habits, which begin from within and is seen without. Godliness or holiness is not talked about very much except in a critical way. Thank God for grace and mercy, however we need to show our gratitude by being committed to holiness when it hurts and when it doesn't. We are ambassadors for Christ. Who shall abide in the tabernacle and dwell in the holy hill? Read Psalm 15. Take time to be holy; spend time with God each day--no T.V., no radio, just quiet time. Do all to the glory of God! Let's get real!

LET'S GET REAL

HYPOCRISY – ENVIES

A hypocrite is one who acts or talks one way to hide his real motive or feelings. He presents a face and behavior different from what is truly in his heart and what he really believes. His motives are for his own profit or benefit, not for the glory of God.

I remember during my childhood, the words "two-faced" were commonly used for one who was hypocritical. We didn't know at that time the meaning was the same as "hypocrite." All I knew was someone would be all smiles and kind in my face and when they were with someone else he/she was unkind or back-biting in word or deed. The Bible uses the phrase "double-minded," one who is unstable in all his ways. Romans chapter 12 verse 9 declares we should love without pretense. An inconsistent Christian grieves the Holy Spirit.

Envy causes one to be hypocritical or two-faced because it complains that it does not have what another has; and it desires wrongfully what others have without regards to the rights of another. It will cause one to pretend to love or care for others in order to befriend them. When we envy, we accuse God of being unfair and say He should've done for me what He did for someone else. If we count our blessings (and we could never count them all), there would be no room for envy.

God blesses us according to His riches in glory and obedience for He is a God of no respect of persons. God is faithful and just. We can depend on Him to supply all of our needs and many of our desires, if we trust Him. Saints, let's be real in private and in public. Remember, we can do nothing of ourselves. Pray sincerely that God will remove these strongholds, among others, and we can grow spiritually and physically. Let's get real!

LET'S GET REAL

JEALOUSY

Jealousy can be defined as (1) demanding complete devotion, (2) untrustingly watchful and (3) the rage of man. Jealousy is one of the oldest sins of the world. It is a type of bondage. One example of jealousy is when Cain slew his brother Abel because Cain's work was evil and Abel's was righteous (I John 3:12).

There are many other instances in the Bible where jealousy caused destruction to self and others. It stunts growth in the spiritual realm and also in the natural. One who is jealous becomes self-centered. Lucifer (Satan) because of his jealousy was thrown out of heaven down to his present position as the prince of the power of the air or ruler of darkness. He wanted to me higher than the Most High God.

How does jealousy gain entrance in our lives? One way is to want what someone else has and not being able to attain it. These deadly seeds began to grow when we aren't watchful. If they are not uprooted, they grow larger and larger until one's life is dominated to a greater degree. Some other spirits related to jealousy are strife, revenge, spite, envy, hatred, cruelty, extreme competition and sometimes murder. One of Satan's main jobs is to sow discord, which is one of the six things that God hates most (Proverbs 6: 19).

As Satan realizes the weakness of jealousy and related emotions, he directs specific strongmen to take advantage of that sin. When we notice any of these spirits working in our lives, we should take action immediately through prayer in the name of Jesus.

Matthew 7:20 tells us that we are known by the fruits that we bear, corruptible or incorruptible. The love of God is the only way to overcome the spirit of jealousy. They that are of Christ have crucified the flesh with affections of lust. When jealousy is harbored, it keeps one from being all he or she can be, especially in the body of Christ.

Let us not be desirous of vainglory (praise of men) provoking and envying one another. One of the main reasons for division in relationships, especially marriages, is the spirit of jealousy. Don't get jealous because God uses one in a different way than he uses the other. We are one body with many members and talents having the same purpose; to serve Jesus Christ. Jealousy, also as anger, causes one to hate what or who is to be admired.

We must be willing to be used by God, however, there are times when God will use someone whether they want to be used or not. Remember the story of Jonah? Ephesians 5:12 tells us to walk in love as followers of God, as dear children and love as Christ loved us and has given Himself for us; an offering and a sacrifice to God for a sweet smelling savor. Jealousy is one of the sins Jesus took to the cross.

It is no secret what God can do; what he has done for others, He'll do for you. Remember, where there is envy and strife there is confusion and every evil work, and God is not a God of confusion. So let's get real!

LEADERSHIP

A leader directs or guides. He/she is also an example. A leader's purpose is to keep order, pursue peace without compromising the truth, and teach the flock how to prosper in the will of God, among other duties.

Moses is one great leader who comes to mind at this time. He was involved with the people, and they with him. Remember the story of how he led the Israelites through the wilderness and came so close to the promised-land, but only got a look at it because of his unbelief (Numbers 20:8-12)? God told him to do one thing and he did another.

Two main requirements of a leader are faith and strength. A weak leader is like having no leader. It is their duty to teach us how to prosper and it is God's will that we prosper in health and otherwise. The more word we get into our hearts the more our souls will prosper. It's not always about money. We can be rich in love, joy, peace, etc.

Leaders must realize that the larger the ministry, the more the problems. Different levels mean different devils. A good leader knows how to handle rejection without alienating affection.

One thing God hates is a proud look (Proverbs 6:17). Many flock members would be dead if looks could kill. I hear many members say they're afraid to speak certain things because of the leader's proud look. Sometimes it is just a sincere facial expression. Many people don't know the difference between bold with confidence and boldness with arrogance.

A leader must be counseled sometimes as well as others. "Where no counsel is the people fall, but in the multitude of counselors there is safety" (Proverbs 11:14). He should not mind being corrected in love. No one knows it all.

A church leader seeks to win souls for Christ and build up God's kingdom, which is what we should be about. Difficult decisions must be made sometimes that don't please everyone; but still there is to be no respect of persons (This is a problem in many churches).

The leader should love his wife as Christ loves the Church in private as well as in public. The Bible also states he must rule his own house well or how can he rule the house of God (I Timothy 3:4). Servants of the Lord mustn't strive but be gentle with all men (II Timothy 2:24). He should feed the flock willingly, be an example, and vehicle for unity.

Jesus is the only one who should be exalted in the church. Many leaders begin with God but end up in self; a very dangerous mistake. If we're Christians we're all leaders in some way, but more authority has been given to some than others. The main leaders of the Church, other than Christ, are the pastor, deacons and trustees. They should cooperate on one accord for the church to prosper.

The church body can go no further than the leader takes it. Yes, leaders are human but in my opinion, they are to be different in some ways. Jesus was different; that's why His own people rejected and killed him. He is the greatest example of a leader.

LET'S GET REAL

Sometimes many excuses are made for not doing or doing certain things, but the fact remains a leader cannot lead when he is behind. A true leader does not run when problems arise. Let's pray for those in leadership. If you think they're not right, look in the glass and make sure you're right and God will take care of the rest. Also, be mindful that an obedient, faithful follower will make a great leader. None is perfect but that doesn't mean we don't strive to be, until we enter that perfect side called Heaven. So, let's get real!

LIGHT OF THE WORLD

Who is the light of the world? Jesus is the light. He came to destroy injustice and unrighteousness. In this world's court, many are freed that should be punished and many are punished who should be freed. In God's government, there is equality (fairness). He is the light because he shows us where we are, where we ought to be and puts us on the right path to get there; the path of righteousness.

Jesus came to enlarge the church by destroying the devil's kingdom. Believers are to be followers of that light. In John 9:5, Jesus said to his disciples, "I am the light of the world." He then proved His statement by healing a blind man.

How are we proving that we are the light or followers of it? Jesus is the light of God and being heirs and joint heirs, we are also. The disciples did the works that Christ did. Jesus came to heal, comfort, deliver, set free and be a planter; to make us trees of righteousness (Isaiah 61:3); children of God, who represent Him and His glory, also to offer total dependence upon Him. Because of God's righteous acts, whatever we are and whatever we have, He made us and gave it to us. If we are strong and steadfast, we owe it all to our Redeemer. Therefore, we should be helping others reach their divine destiny.

When the Israelites were in a sad, hopeless state, Christ was their light. He gave them joy, hope and happiness so they could be trees of righteousness and now we must get up, go out and win souls for Christ by doing for someone else what He has done for us. No time for pity parties, feeling sorry for yourself or a lot complaining which does no good anyway.

There are many ways to let our light shine as vessels for God. Be sure we're walking what we talk. Jesus said in this world, we will have tribulations, but still the light must shine. We're overcomers and more than conquerors and haven't done anything to deserve it.

Let others see Jesus in you. Without Him, we're spiritually blind, walking in total darkness. If you're not saved, then sin is separating you from God. If you leave this world not knowing Jesus Christ, hell is your eternal home. <u>The</u> Light, not <u>a</u> light, frees us from guilt and despair; for God is faithful and just to forgive our sins and cleanse us from all unrighteousness if we confess our sins (I John 1:9). While you have light, believe in The Light (spiritual light) that you may be children of the light (John 12:36). If we, as children of light, take control of our thoughts, tongue, and temper, many times our light will shine instead of darkness.

Let me leave you with this anecdote of how to stay focused on the church. Christ is the head and all grace and strength comes from Him. *Amazing grace, how sweet the sound, that saved a wretch like me. I once was lost, but now I'm found; was blind, but now I see.* Aren't you glad that you can see? Thank God for the Redeemer, The Light of the World! Let's get real!

LOVE THY NEIGHBOR

Who is love? God is love. Who is God? God is the Creator, Maker, Ruler, and potter of the heavens and earth and all that dwells therein. He is real. If we say we love God and hate our brother or sister, we walk in darkness and the love of God does not dwell within us.

Love is an action word. It is easy to say, "I love you," but do our actions coincide (agree with) our words? Love works no evil to his neighbor (Romans 13:10). Who is thy neighbor? A neighbor is any member of the human race that we come in contact with. The Bible tells us to love the Lord thy God with all thine heart, thy mind, soul and strength and love thy neighbor as thyself (Lev. 19:18; Matt. 19:19).

Mark chapter 12 verse 23 tells us that love is better than sacrifice. Love is forgiveness, patience, kindness, humility and discipline. Love is showing charity towards the most unlovable person. Love shows respect and tolerance for others. Many times it is necessary to put others before self. Charity is giving honor to whomever it is due. Charity condescends to those of low estate. Love your enemies, for if you love only those who love you, what reward have ye (Matthew 5:46)?

How do I love my unknown enemy? Well, the Bible tells us to be kind to all men, even strangers; especially to those of the household of faith. By doing so we may entertain angels unaware and if we are kind to all without partiality, our unknown enemy will be included. This will serve to heap coals upon the heads of our enemies (Romans 12:9).

Love allows one to be his or herself. Love is not easily angered, easily provoked, selfish, envious, or puffed up (I Corinthians 13:4/5). Charity does not alienate affection due to differences in personality or opinion. We owe no man anything except to love one another (Romans 13:10).

What if God had not loved us enough to give His only begotten son that whosoever believeth on Him shall not perish but have everlasting life (John

3:16)? Additionally what if he didn't overlook our faults and supply our needs? There are many ways to show love. Let us not love with dissimulation (pretense), but in actions and in truth. I say to you: Husbands, love your wives unconditionally. Wives love your husbands unconditionally. Parents love your children unconditionally. Children love your parents unconditionally. Love thy neighbor unconditionally; for love is the more excellent way! God bless and let's get real!

PEACE

There are several definitions for "peace." I think of peace as being the calmness of thought, speech, actions or reactions when everything around you is in turmoil or chaos. Peace is contentment and freedom from anxiety.

First Peter 3:11 tells us to seek peace and pursue it. One way is by doing good deeds instead of evil. The peace of God which passes all understanding shall keep our hearts and minds through Christ Jesus (Philippians 4:7). The world cannot understand this kind of peace and some saints don't seem to understand it.

When everything seems to be going wrong, we can be happy and joyous because we know that God is working something out on our behalf. There is peace in knowing that the Lord will make ways that we can't see. He will open doors that no one can close; or close doors that no one can open. He can do what no one else can do. I personally have experienced that when challenged with problems that threatened my peace in the home, in school, or the job and especially the church.

Keep your mind on Jesus and the God of peace will always be with you. Don't concentrate on the circumstances or situation. Use your ESP (Express Something Powerful)--God's word! For example: "With God on my side I will make it." Or "I can do all things through Christ which strengthens me." Or "When I am afraid I will trust in the Lord." Or "The Lord is my strong tower in the time of storm." Abide in the word and let it abide in you and what seems to be an obstacle will turn out to be an opportunity. What seems to be bad, God will work it out for your good.

Sometimes to keep peace one must be quiet and keep thoughts to oneself. The Bible tells us to live peaceably with all men as much as lies within us. That doesn't mean to compromise God's word. Let's get it together saints, and strive for peace with all, not just friends or those in our circle.

There are times when we have no peace because we are not as prayerful as we should be.

Mark 4:39 tells us about the disciples being in the boat on the water and a storm came. They were afraid. The boat was filled with water. Jesus was asleep, at peace. He was awakened and He rebuked the wind and said to the sea "Peace, be still!" There was a great calm (peace).

When we are going through storms in our lives, we need to learn how to be still or silent. I've had many storms and rain in my life, but by the grace and mercy of God I made it. I didn't know the Lord then. Now, whatever He allows me to experience I have that inner peace, knowing that He is in it. I am His and He is mine and I welcome the peace that I receive from His promise. My soul is anchored in the peace of God for He is the God of life, breath, and all things. Without him we have no being. So peace I leave with you. Let's get real.

RESURRECTION

The visit to the tomb by the women on the morning of Christ's resurrection reflects a custom observed during that time, which was the anointing of the body of a deceased person, who in this case was Jesus. Yet, it also was an indication of deep misunderstanding or a lack of faith in the words of Jesus. He said on one occasion "Destroy this temple and in three days I will raise it up." We as believers know He was not talking about a building. The women went not expecting to see Him raised, but to anoint His body. They wondered who would roll the stone away that they might reach the body of Jesus.

After entering the sepulcher and not finding the body of Jesus, but seeing a young man at the right side clothed in a white garment they were affrighted. The young man told them to go and tell the disciples and Peter that He had risen. Special emphasis was put on telling Peter because he had denied Christ and this message would be a great comfort and reassure him of Christ's love for him.

The resurrection of Jesus is the foundation on which Christianity is built. Paul declares in I Corinthians 15:17 "If Christ be not raised, your faith is vain and ye are yet in your sins." Romans 1:4 states "And declared to be the Son of God with power, according to the Spirit of holiness by the resurrection from the dead."

Being adopted into God's family we receive the privileges and responsibilities of son-ship along with God's eternal Son, Jesus. Many Christians are eager to receive the privileges of son-ship but are adverse in assuming its responsibilities. Christ does not ask us to do anything that He has not done. "Let this mind be in you, which was also in Christ Jesus." Saints, let's get real!

LET'S GET REAL

RUTH AND NAOMI (FAMILY LOVE)

Ruth pledged her love and devotion to Naomi and the God of Israel. Naomi left the house of praise to escape change. Naomi went to a place called Moab (the world). Because of her disobedience tragedy after tragedy occurred. Naomi and Ruth (her daughter-in-law) went back to Bethlehem to an uncertain future. This was an example of a strong family bond, a strong marriage and a strong relationship between Christ and the church.

Naomi was a Christian woman but she and her husband still had worldly things in them. When God began to judge and deal with them, they left the house of God.

There are those who yield to dealings and grow. Some go so far, but there are areas that they don't want to give up, so they go back into the world, wanting nothing to do with God.

Whatever is coming between you and God, get it right and keep it right. Don't be hard on yourself and don't condemn yourself. Just let God have his way in that particular area of your life.

Psalm 66:12 states that everything God allows is so that we can go deeper in him. God is always right, no matter what we go through, so we need to give him praise. Why don't we give him praise right now!!!

Naomi makes a plan for Ruth to have a better life or future. Ruth didn't mind because Ruth did it out of love for Naomi, not Boaz. They were committed to one another. Ruth's love was so strong for Naomi, that she didn't care what others thought about what she did at the threshing floor.

Let's look at their accomplishments. They had excellent relationships. Their greatest bond was faith in God. Also they had a mutual commitment; each did what was best for the other.

Lessons from their lives: God's presence in a relationship overcomes differences that might cause disharmony or divisions; differences such as culture, family background or age. They were a good example of blending lives, a healthy marriage and Christ and the church.

They shared deep sorrow, had affection for each other and an overriding commitment to the God of Israel. They depended on each other. Jesus said if we are to follow him, we must deny ourselves, take up our cross and follow him. When we begin to cross out and purge our lives, then we begin to live a resurrected life (in the mind). Attitude, disposition, and character change. Then we can experience the kingdom of God at all times.

Certain things have been put in our minds from the world that keep us from experiencing the kingdom of God; which is peace, righteousness and joy in the Holy Ghost. God still has to consume some things out of us. So let's get real!

SELFLESS LOVE VS LIKE

To like means to have pleasure in or to be pleased with. Love means to be concerned about the needs of others, giving up your rights, feelings and preferences sometimes and allowing one to be who he/she is; giving when it hurts (sacrifice); going two miles with your brethren when you're only asked to go one.

Many times I hear the phrase "I love you, but don't like you." In my opinion, most of the time love is not involved in that statement. The statement is used for an excuse to avoid certain people. Maybe there is a reason to shun sometimes.

The Bible says to let your light shine in darkness. Sometimes one isn't liked because of social status, personality, disagreement or just because they aren't the way we want them to be. Do we really understand how to love one and not like what he or she does? Can we overlook agitating habits without retaliating and still love?

We don't have to know one to express love in

the Lord. God may use your enemy to help you see certain attributes of yourself that need purging. The people who you think you don't like may be being used by God. The Bible says love your enemy and sometimes love begins with "like." Love is not going another way to keep from speaking. It is an action word, shown as well as spoken. As a child I used to hear "I love you, but not what you do." It took me a while to understand that.

What if parents put children away because they didn't like them but loved them? Think about that statement. I don't like being around foul language or riotous behavior, but if I can supply a need in the will of God, I will. Remember, God's ways are not our ways and neither are His thoughts our thoughts, but do we like Him and not love Him? I know that sounds like a foolish question but think about it. God made us all different for various reasons, in personality and otherwise–all for His purpose, realizing some differences are of self.

Sometimes we don't like because of jealousy, envy or even malice. Where do you stand? Do you like only those who act and think as you or those in your circle? Thank God for those who you think you love and those you think you don't like. Ephesians 5:20 states, "…always giving thanks for all things, unto God and the Father in the name of our Lord Jesus Christ." Think positive about those you don't like and you feel different towards. Try it! That is part of renewing the mind–seeing good and not always looking for bad.

If God is the head of your life, realize sometimes that He puts people in your path. It doesn't have to be an enemy and know that if we love Him, He's working for our good. Check your motives for loving but not liking and be sure it isn't the person, but their sinful ways. The Bible says, love the sinner, but hate the sin. There is some good in everyone and everything God made was good. It just went bad and can be restored.

Let us live as servants of God that with well doing, we may put to silence the ignorance of foolish men (I Peter 2:15). Let's get real!

SPIRIT OF FEAR

Fear can be positive or negative. The fear of God is the beginning of wisdom; positive (Psalm 111:10). Obey God's commandments and respect Him just because He is who He is. I respect electricity because I know it will harm me or possibly kill me. This is positive fear.

The first appearance of fear in the world was after Adam and Eve sinned. "I heard thy voice in the garden and I was afraid," was Adam's response when God asked "where art thou" (Genesis 3:10). God did not give us the spirit of fear, but of power, of love, and of a sound mind (II Timothy 1:7).

Negative fear destroys joy, peace, faith and love. It weakens the Christian, giving way for other spirits such as bondage or infirmities. Fear is a type of bondage. Jesus recognized the disciples' fear while they were battling the storm as a lack of faith. "Why are you fearful, O ye of little faith (Matthew 8:26)?

Of course we know it is impossible to please

Him without faith. Fear is torment. Love cannot have its perfect work in us if we fear. Negative fear is when we believe what the devil says more than God's word. Fear is opposed to God's laws. The Bible tells us to fear not what man can do to us, but fear the one who can harm the body and soul in hell, which is Jesus.

    As I talk with others, many are fearful of standing up as witnesses, especially in the household of faith. If we can't be free in the house of God, where can we be free? For he who the Son sets free is free indeed. I do realize we all are in different stages of growth. I certainly am still growing in all areas of the Lord. We can't move until we make a move. How do we overcome this fear, or any fear? By letting God's word be our guide. Fill our hearts and minds with His word which is the sword. Pray it, sing it, or speak it.

    Some may think it is normal to fear. Maybe that's true for sinners because when one walks in disobedience to God, he is open season. Anything can happen. But it is not normal for God's children to fear for he never leaves us nor forsakes us.

The scripture tells us that whosoever denies Jesus before men, him will He deny before the Father which is in heaven. God wants strong, courageous soldiers. He will strengthen us and though we may fall, we will not be utterly cast down for He will uphold us with his righteous hand. No weapon formed against us will prosper and any tongue that rises against us thou shall condemn, for this is the heritage of the saints. Pray the prayer of faith for God to deliver you from fear or any other hindrance.

A few years ago, I was under attack by enemies. I had no fear because I knew the battle was His and He fought it. Psalm 27 became one of my inspirational scriptures and I gained spiritual strength as a result of that experience. However, victory was mine.

This is a stricken world! However, remember God is still in control and nothing or no one can touch a hair on your head unless He permits it, for He desires our good. Let us be effective, bold witnesses for our Father wherever we go and remember that whatever is bound on earth is bound in heaven and whatever is loosed on earth is loosed in heaven. We are the salt of the earth and if we lose the savor we are nothing. **We are the light of the world; the head and not the tail. God is our helper, so let's get real!**

SPIRIT OF HUMILITY

Humility is depending totally on God; realizing we're nothing without Him. It is the attitude of a servant (Eph. 4: 1-3). Humility is joy, putting Jesus first, others next and then yourself.

Humility is a vital characteristic for a Christian. Some other characteristics related to humility are mercy, kindness, meekness, a quiet spirit, and humbleness of mind (not thinking more highly of yourself than you ought Phil. 2: 3/4). God gives grace to the humble but resists the proud. The greatest of all is charity (Col. 3:12-14).

Why is humility stressed? (1) When Christ was on the cross, He exhibited humility and love, which is what kept Him on the cross. (2) Because of His grace, mercy, kindness, and love, regardless of our works, are reasons we should desire the Spirit of humility.

Without the Spirit of humility, we have no real walk with God, nor fellowship, nor working of the Holy Spirit. Without the Spirit of humility, we usually do things our own way. We never arrive at complete humility.

Paul stated that I am a prisoner of the Lord (Eph. 4:1). This meant that he had no more rights because he was a servant of god. He was a great example of Jesus, the suffering servant that Isaiah 53 talks about. He was consecrated to God just as we who are called by His name should be. II Chronicles 7:14 says, "If my people which are called by my name, shall humble themselves, pray, and seek my face and turn from their wicked ways; then will I hear from heaven, forgive their sins and will heal their land." He that has an ear to hear let him hear.

Don't be too proud to admit you can't make it without Christ, or to come to Him and admit that you can't handle it. Surrender all to him; family, friends, foes, fears, and faults. We must die to self; including our thoughts. We must be able to suffer for a just cause for Christ and persevere during difficult times.

Humility is all about Jesus. We are blessed that he chose us sealed until the day of redemption

(Eph. 7:9/11). We should be able to say as Paul says; I've fought a good fight, I have finished my course and kept the faith and to live is Christ (II Tim. 4:7). Humble yourselves under the mighty hand of God and He will exalt you in due time. **My sisters and brothers, live in Christ. Let's get real!**

SPIRIT OF TRUTH

What is truth? One definition given is "that which agrees with final reality and is right and certain." Truth is the opposite of a lie. God's word is truth (John 17:17). It is right, certain and definitely a reality. John 8:32 states "and you shall know the truth and the truth shall make you free." Therefore, we are able ministers of the New Testament, not of the letter, for the letter kills, but the Spirit gives life (II Cor. 3:6). So we must worship God in sincerity and truth (I Cor. 5:8). If He is not worshipped from the heart, all is vain.

God delights in a person of truth, but a lying tongue is an abomination (detest, despise) to Him (Proverbs 12:22). One who speaks the truth sows forth righteousness (Proverbs 12:17). Speak truth regardless of negative consequences. A person of truth is not liked very much. Only a mature sister or brother can handle or admire one of truth, rather than get angry at him or her.

Many times we speak what pleases man to get

what or where we want, instead of trusting God and speaking what pleases Him. Speak the truth in love. We can't be free if we always hear what we want to hear instead of what we ought to hear. The truth helps us to see things in ourselves we don't want to see or admit. Everyone is not going to like you whether you speak truth or lies. So why not speak what the Lord says, being certain it is He who is speaking to you. Family, friends, and even foes will leave you alone, but fret not because God gives you who and what you need to carry out the given task. Woe unto him who is liked by all men.

The Bible says anyway, we are to love one another, not "like," if we are to enter the Kingdom of God. The truth hurts sometimes therefore we will not acknowledge or face the truth. When making an important decision, there is no peace or freedom of mind until it is done. So make a decision to be one of truth. You're in man's favor as long as you please him. Jesus was a man of truth. He was rejected, hated, lied on and crucified; so we shouldn't expect anything different. He said in this world, we will have tribulation. But be of good cheer, He has overcome! And knowing He has overcome, we are overcomers. When we make people believe we are what we're not, we are living an untruth.

I'm reminded of the story of the prophet Micah and Ahab, the evil King (I Kings 15-23). Micah was hated by the king because he didn't tell the king what he wanted to hear, as other prophets, but spoke what "thus said the Lord." Sometimes truth means standing alone except with Jesus. Therefore, gird up your loins with truth (Ephesians 6:14). Know the source of your information and put away lying. Speak every man truth with his neighbor for we are members one of another (Ephesians 4:25).

God loves you and can use you in spite of your shortcomings. Come to Him and repent (change your ways and be truly sorry). He will forgive. It is not always about ability but availability. So let's worship God in spirit and in truth from the heart. In short, let's get real!

LET'S GET REAL

STUBBORNNESS-REBELLION

Stubbornness is an expression of self-will. It is as idolatry and causes one to ignore the voice of God (I Sam. 15:23 and Deut. 21:18). Choosing to obey a lesser "god"—Satan. Rebellion, a very close kin to stubbornness, is as witchcraft. Other related ideas are anger, fear, backsliding, and disobedience.

When Jesus said, "Take this cup from me," that was the human side speaking. But in submission to God, He said, "Not my will, but thy will be done." This is what we should say when that stubborn seed begins to rise up in us, especially when things don't seem to be going our way.

The Holy Spirit reminds us when we're getting ready to say or do something out of character. It is up to us to listen to that still small voice or override it and do what the flesh says to do. "Therefore if any man be in Christ, he is a new creature. Old things are passed away; behold all things are become new" (II Cor. 5:17). Our will is transformed to God's will.

Stubbornness can be positive and negative. An example: if someone is trying to pervert your faith or entreat you to go against the will of God, that's a good time to be stubborn. That's when your spiritual wisdom steps in. Stubbornness can be a very harmful fruit. It will prevent one or a group from excelling in the natural and supernatural. We may think others can't see it, but God sees where we can't. Sometimes, it takes fasting and prayer to break or destroy yokes in our lives.

Because of stubbornness, some will obey who they like rather than one of truth. If any be a hearer of the word and not a doer, he deceives himself. He is like unto a man beholding his natural face in a glass and going away forgetting what manner of man he was (James 1:22-24). Many leaders fall because of stubbornness. Where no counsel is, the people fall; but in the multitude of counselors, there is safety (Prov. 11-14).

Pride is also a form of stubbornness and is an abomination to the Lord; for He gives grace to the humble and resists the proud (James 4:6). Also pride goes before destruction and a haughty spirit before a fall (Prov. 16:18). Replace stubbornness with humility which comes before honor (Prov. 15:33). To remove this ungodly trait from your life, ask God to forgive and remember whatever is bound on earth is bound in heaven. Whatsoever is loosed on earth is loosed in heaven (Matt. 18:18). Everything we need is in the word of God. So let's get real and god bless.

SUFFERING

As we know, suffering is a very broad subject. I could never tell even half of it. Suffering is a part of love; for God gave His only begotten Son to suffer for us because He loved us. Jesus said "In the world you will have tribulation" (John 16:33). He was giving us a realistic view of the world.

He spoke from personal experience. He bore our griefs and carried our sorrows (Isaiah 53:3). He knew what it was like to be misunderstood by loved ones; to be rejected by his family and closest followers. He was betrayed, hated and abandoned. He was verbally and physically abused. He experienced many other types of suffering. Yet it was suffering that kept his eyes on heaven; showing us what we believe is all important. Jesus said if we abide in his word, we are his disciples indeed. And you shall know the truth and the truth shall make you free (John 8:31-32).

My friends, if we are to be followers of Christ, we must deny ourselves, take up our cross and follow Him, for we are called to be sufferers. Therefore, He must increase and we must decrease. We are not our own. We are bought and paid for. He paid it all by shedding His blood on the cross. By His stripes we are healed.

Because of his suffering, there is deliverance. We have victory through faith in Jesus. Many characters in the Bible suffered for Christ's sake. Namely, Paul and Stephen were great sufferers. Now saints, we must learn to suffer and count it all joy, for Christ will, with the affliction, give us strength to endure because He said He will never leave nor forsake us. Many times we experience suffering to strengthen us in faith, or so that Jesus will manifest Himself through us. Perhaps one can even learn to be strong through another's suffering.

Suffering is also sometimes a result of sin. Remember the Bible tells us we reap what we sow or what we measure out will be measured back to us. During suffering, Jesus is sometimes molding and shaping us into what He wants us to be. Self-examination can reveal positive blessings in our lives.

Why do we suffer? Suffering proves. It is in His plan to prove our faith. If faith goes, everything goes. If faith stands, everything stands. Malachi 3:3 tells us about purification through suffering. Christ is too good to allow anything to touch you that won't work for your good. Romans 8:28 tells us and we know that all things work together for good to them that love the Lord.

And remember, Satan cannot touch a hair on your head without Christ's permission; sometimes to try our faith. Many times Christians see their trials and temptations as being of the devil. He does bring about much that hurts us, but Christ is over him also.

Paul said in Philippians 1:6, "He which hath begun a good work in you will perform it." That is, He will finish it and you will come forth as pure gold. Sometimes we bare needless pains because we don't take our cares and concerns to God in prayers. We are priests and Kings, therefore we should not be bound, for Christ has set us free and he who the Son has set free, is free indeed. Whatever the need, He will supply it on time. Whatever the problem, He will solve it on time. Maybe not in our time or our way, but it will certainly be done, for He is an on-time God.

When it seems like trouble is on every side, battles and fears without and within, be encouraged because He will never leave nor forsake you. Let us show our love and gratitude for His love by keeping His commandments to love the Lord thy God with all our heart, mind, soul and strength and be loving, kind, and forgiving of one another. The doctor may leave you but not the Great Physician; your loved ones may grow weary as they wait on you, but not the Lord. They may slumber or sleep, but He won't. He feels whatever we feel, suffers whatever we suffer. Nothing touches us without touching Him first.

Men, women, boys and girls, learn to suffer patiently; for it is through much tribulation that we will enter the kingdom of God (Acts 14:22). Let's be real!

THE JOY OF GIVING

Giving is an act of love (John 3:16). There are many scriptures in the Bible regarding giving. II Corinthians 9:6-7 declares if we give sparingly, we will receive sparingly. If we give bountifully we receive bountifully, and give not grudgingly or out of necessity, but according as every man purposed in his heart.

God loves a cheerful giver whether your time, talent, gift or money. He wants us to give wholeheartedly. Giving is a way of worshiping God. Freely we have received, freely we are to give. We do not give, or should not, expecting to receive from whom we give; for our reward may possibly come through someone or something else. The Bible states if we have worldly goods and see our brethren in need and do not help him/her, how can the love of God dwell in us (I John 3:7)?

Let me share a short testimony with you. Several years ago we had an obligation to make two house payments and a car payment. It was not easy;

we had to make changes in our life style but didn't neglect to pay tithes and offerings. It wasn't that we had lots of money, but we realized obedience is better than sacrifice. We also had a ministry involving money. I almost gave it up, but the Spirit reminded me of the scripture that says "Give and it shall be given unto you, shaken together, pressed down and running over. . ." So we continued. This was not told to exalt us in any way but to exalt my heavenly Father who provided and watched over us. All glory and honor goes to Him!

Bring ye all the tithes and offerings into the store house and see if I will not open the windows of heaven and pour you out a blessing that there will not be room enough to receive it (Malachi 3:10). He has done that for my husband and me in more ways than one. If God doesn't do anything else, He has already blessed us above and beyond our highest expectation, but He's not through with us yet. No matter how little you think you have, bless someone else who is less fortunate than you and experience the JOY OF GIVING; for we reap whatsoever we sow.

LET'S GET REAL

Let's get real!

LET'S GET REAL

THE LORD IS MY SHEPHERD

The Shepherd is one who cares for his sheep and will give his life for them (John 10:11). Do we have any real Shepherds today? He defends them and is fearless (I Samuel 17:34-36); he gives rest (Jeremiah 33:12); and is faithful (Genesis 31:38-40). He must be strong because his sheep depend totally upon him.

Because the Lord is my Shepherd, I don't have to want, worry or fret. Because He is my Shepherd, I know he will provide and some things have been laid up for me that I didn't work for. Sometimes when I don't know which way to go and my path seems dark, He is not only my Shepherd, but also my light and my salvation (Psalms 27:1).

We have been loaded with benefits and privileges but we must receive them. He gives me peace that the world can't achieve nor understand and leads me in the path of righteousness for His name's sake. No matter how difficult or dangerous things may seem, I can have contentment. When I lay down at night, I can be at ease because if my Shepherd is for me, He assures me that He is greater than those who are against me.

When I am sick he heals my body, renews my strength and restores my soul. He keeps me, He is my redeemer, and never leaves or forsakes me. This I must remember whenever I face a problem or trial. Because my Shepherd is in control, Satan can't do anything, until the Shepherd finishes with me.

He came to give life and give it more abundantly, to bless me with overflow in body and soul. He's meat when I'm hungry, drink when I'm thirsty. His word and Spirit shall comfort me. He has prepared a table for me before my enemies and they couldn't understand it.

If I don't have what I desire at the time I desire it, I've learned that it isn't for me or not time for it because He is an on-time Shepherd. He promised if I delight myself in Him, he would give me the desires of my heart. I may fall or fail but I don't have to stay down, because this is the confidence that I have in Him–If I call on Him, He will hear.

Even though I go through the valley of the shadow of death I can be at ease. It is just a shadow and no great evil is in it. His yoke is easy and His burden is light. Death cannot separate me from the love of my Shepherd (Romans 8:38). It harms the body but not my soul. We can't live life to the fullest in fear.

We who are in Christ will be moved to a better world when we have done all that the Shepherd has for us to do in this present world. That place is where there are many mansions; the house of the Lord. There will be no more sickness, sorrow, tears or troublesome things of this world. This Shepherd is the great I AM. All we need is in Him. Do you know this Shepherd? I encourage you to seek Him. Let's get real!

UNIQUE

What is the meaning of unique: (1) One of its kind and (2) uncommon or rare? As I walk, ride, or just sit, I observe different types of people--all sizes, colors, shapes and different personalities. Sometimes I see look-a-likes, but even though they look alike, speak in the same manner or even dress alike, I can tell there is a difference in their thoughts by their actions. For we are each God's unique creation; forming one uniqueness in the Spirit, the Body of Christ. Believers are to be different. God created us for His divine purpose to use our time, talents, and gifts for the edification and encouragement of one another.

We should not try to mimic another nor attempt to change anyone into what or who we think they ought to be. One definition for love is to allow one to be who he/she is. Christ accepted us just as we were and we should accept others the same. We should pray for them, for God is the only one who knows what, how and when to change, not we ourselves for He made us.

We can disagree without disrespecting and alienating affection for one another. In spite of our differences in opinions and ways, we must love unconditionally. We're not in the profession alone. We're laborers with God and every time we help someone else, we're helping ourselves.

Together we make up a church of God's handiwork or masterpiece. The Spirit of God has made us (Job 33:4), so we must worship Him in spirit and in truth. I heard someone say meekness is Jesus the lion with the spirit of a lamb. Let us be an example. May we all prosper and be in health as our souls prosper. Let's be real!

UNITY

What is unity: (1) joining together as to form one connected whole, (2) to join in action, interest, opinion or feeling. Psalms 133 states how good and pleasant it is for brethren to dwell together in unity. Who are brethren? Church members…I think not. It is referring to believers or born again saints.

Christ prayed for his disciples that they would be one as He and the Father are one, and that they would be one in them. The same applies to us today who are believers. This oneness gives us freedom today. There is strength and power in unity. Where there is harmony, there are heavenly blessings. Where there is disunity, there is despair. There is no room for jealousy in keeping harmony. The Bible also tells us where there is envying and strife, there is every evil work. Understanding is also very important in keeping unity. So let's get it together Household of Faith, especially in our church meetings.

LET'S GET REAL

We are all unique in our own way. We don't all think, talk, or even look alike. And even though we don't pray, teach or preach in the same fashion, hopefully we have the same intentions; to win souls for Christ and to stay in tune with our heavenly Father. In a unity of spirit, we are a family, one with each other and one with God. If we maintain our unity with God, the gates of hell cannot prevail against us. It doesn't matter what denomination, color, or nationality, we are one in Christ.

Thank God there are no little you's and big I's, nor little I's and big you's in Christ. The church should stick together. Then we can do all things through Christ that strengthens us. Husband and wife should be as one or their prayers will be hindered. Family and communities should stick together. The closer we get to Christ, the closer we will get to one another. The scripture tells us where two agree as touching on earth; whatever we ask, we will receive.

Be in unity with me in these areas in prayer. I pray for unity in the church, for judgment will begin there and if we can't get it right within, how can we help get it right without; something to think about. I also pray for minds to be renewed, that healing and deliverance will take place in the household of faith more than ever. Also I pray for heavy burdens to be undone. Most of all that we will be more diligent in seeking souls for Christ. Thank you for your unity in prayer. Let's be sure that as unifiers, we are walking in the right direction. When we walk in unity, we are helpers, not hindrances. Unity!! There is nothing like it, so let's get real!

UNITY OF BELIEVERS

Behold, how good and pleasant it is for brethren (believers) to dwell together in unity (togetherness) (Psalms 133:1). For there to be unity, we must have the mind of Christ. Seek his desires, not our own. Be ye all of one mind having compassion one to another, be pitiful, love as brethren, and be courteous, not rendering evil for evil or railing for railing but contrariwise blessing; knowing that you are called to inherit a blessing.

For he that will love life and see good days; let him refrain his tongue from evil and his lips that they speak no guile. Let him eschew (avoid or depart from) evil and do good deeds. Let him seek peace and pursue or follow after it; for the eyes of the Lord are upon the righteous and His ears are open to their prayers, but the face of the Lord is against them that do evil (I Peter 3:3-12). How we ought to live is peaceably with all men as much as lies in us (Romans 12:18).

Three important qualities in keeping unity are: love, humility and fellowship. It is significant for leaders to be involved with the people and people with leaders for we are family. However one knows it is almost impossible to live peaceably with some, no matter how hard we try. There is no place for envy, selfishness or jealousy and other related spirits.

The Bible says submit one to another, especially to those in authority and to obey and pray for them. Follow them as they follow Christ. Do not follow those who rebel against authority. Therefore, we must know the word for ourselves. Scripture also says husbands love your wives as Christ loves the church, according to knowledge, giving honor to them as unto the weaker vessel and as being heirs together of the grace of life that your prayers be not hindered and wife reverence your husband.

I can't help but wonder if the church would be in better order if marriages were in order; especially the leaders' marriages. Could it be that a lack of order causes some prayers to be hindered? We are a symbol of Christ and the church; something else to think about. We are the light of the world. So let us walk as children of light, not behaving unseemly (unsaved, unruly, disorderly).

God takes care of his own and whatever should or shouldn't be, He will in His time and way handle it, but we must be obedient to his word. There is not a person in this universe, that doesn't have something about him or her, that isn't likeable. However, it is our responsibility to love even the most unlovable, even our enemy, letting our light shine in all darkness.

God said touch not mine anointed and do my prophets no harm (Psalms 105:150). God will judge His people and vengeance is His. It is a dangerous thing to fall into the hands or wrath of the living God (Hebrews 10:31). Let us strive to be one in mind, spirit and body. We are not our own and we serve Christ by serving each other.

The love I have talked about is agape love, the fervent charity that covers a multitude of sins. This is the strong, sincere, everlasting love that loves one whether he/she is right or wrong, whether you understand or don't. There can be no unity without this kind of love. Whose side are you on? I'm on the Lord's side!

    Finally, my brethren, be strong in the Lord, for divided we fall, together we stand. Let's get real.

WHO DO YOU SERVE AND WHY?

Set your affection on things above where moth, rust and corruption can't set in and thieves and robbers can't break in and steal. Where your treasure is there your heart will be also (Matthew 6:19-21). This scripture tells us that we have something to understand at the beginning of the sentence. You set your mind on things above; love and faithfulness are twin virtues. Where your love lies is where your faithfulness will be also. Seek heavenly things– wisdom, spiritual understanding and knowledge.

Do you have a strong prayer life? Do you ever fast? Are you attending Sunday school regularly, prayer meetings and Bible study and of course Sunday services to hear what God has given to Pastors and other Ministers? Are you making necessary changes to prepare for the future eternal home in heaven? Remember the things of this world are temporary. If this is where all of your joy and delight is, it is foolish; for only a fool will lay up treasure for himself and be not rich toward God

(Luke 2:20-21), who gives us quickly all things to enjoy (I Timothy 6:17).

    If you seek God and his righteousness, all the other things will be added unto you as he sees fit; homes, cars, money, business and even health. As your soul prospers, so will you prosper, and be in good health (II John 4). He wants us to enjoy the things that He has given us, but not put them before Him. Thou shall have no other God before me (Deuteronomy 5:7). One might say I have all the worldly things and don't serve the Lord; but what does a man profit if he shall gain the whole world and lose his own soul (Matthew 16:26)?

    Who do you serve, God or mammon? All prosperity comes from God and it is good to have the results of the blessings, but it is better to have the Blesser. Whether poor or rich we all have something that doesn't belong to us. Do we really realize who we're serving and who we are? If so, let's get rid of the angry, stubborn, rebellious spirits. Get angry, but sin not.

LET'S GET REAL

Stubbornness is idolatry. Rebellion is as witchcraft, all against the will of God. No, I'm not perfect but I am striving and if you know the Lord you should be also. We can disagree and still serve God. Pride and self must go if we are to serve God whole-heartedly and not things and man. Jesus didn't say "ought not" or "should not" but you "cannot" serve two gods. Many are weak and dead as a result of trying to serve two gods or partaking of the Lord's body unworthily (I Cor. 10:21). Think on this: if there were no heaven, no more blessings in store, would you continue to serve Him, praise Him for what he's already done, just because He is God?

I thank God for bringing me out of the authority of darkness into the authority of light. I will serve Him for the rest of my life for He is the firm foundation. The earth is the Lord's and the fullness thereof, the world and they that dwell therein (Psalms 24:1). Choose ye this day who you will serve, as for me and my house we will serve the Lord (Joshua 24:15). Who are you serving–God or mammon–and why? My brothers and sisters, let's get real!

WORRY (WORLDLY CARES)

Two things can cause worry– the past, what's been done and what hasn't been done and future– what might be done. Neither is under our control. It is good to be concerned and caring. God is concerned and He cares in the proper areas. I believe everyone worries at some time or another no matter what the status is but we grow in God's grace in that area just as we do in other areas of our lives.

I used to be an impulsive worrier but thank God since I met Jesus, the majority of it has been taken away. Worry can't heal, solve a problem or supply a need. It only chokes the word (Matthew 13:7/22), obstructs the gospel (Luke 14:18-20), hinders Christ's work (II Timothy 2:4) and manifests unbelief (Matthew 6:25-32). The Bible states take no thought for tomorrow for it will take thought of the things of itself. But seek first the Kingdom of God and His righteousness, and all your need and even your desires will be given to you.

There is nothing too high, low or wide that my Father in heaven can't master. He is the great I AM! Worry makes you sick physically, mentally, emotionally and spiritually. It makes you sad and the joy of the Lord is our strength. Worry will kill quicker than any physical disease if not mastered (controlled).

Some might say worry is one of my weaknesses but if it is not of God, it is wicked or sin. Now I know some things are not a matter of good or bad, but are they profitable? God wants us to profit or be productive. Know you not that your body is the temple of God? Him shall God destroy for the temple of God is Holy (I Cor. 3:17). Worry will certainly destroy the whole body.

If you don't feel like you should, think like it and you will eventually feel how you think, whether physically, emotionally or spiritually. As a man thinks in his heart (mind) so is he. Jesus said in this world we will have tribulations which works patience. Patience is one of Jesus' greatest virtues and must be one of ours also. When problems arise, don't magnify the problem, thinking or talking about it, but magnify the Problem Solver, the Healer, and Deliverer–Jesus!

God made many promises regarding improper concerns. He told us to cast our cares upon Him and leave them there (I Peter 5:7). Then He said he would never leave nor forsake us. Also, be careful for nothing but always pray and always give thanks for if we walk in obedience, He is always working for our good–whether we understand it or not.

Remember, prayer and praise is twin virtues. So put on the garment of praise instead of the spirit of heaviness, especially when going through; for God lives in the praise of His people. In all things we are more than conquerors through Him that loved us (Romans 8:37).

Some of the unhappiest people I know are Christians. Wonder why? Could it be because we are so caught up in our worldly cares or circumstances? Trials determine your level of spiritual faith and strength. Faith is what moves God, not position, titles or education. Learn to thank God for what he hasn't done as much as what He has done, realizing that He knows what is best.

God will give us perfect peace if we keep our hearts and minds on Jesus. This peace the world cannot understand nor take away! The Lord is my shepherd. I don't have to want for anything. Many know the shepherd's psalm but do they know the shepherd-Jesus? Let's get real!

YOU CAN MAKE IT
(A Note to Single Mothers)

Hopefully, this will be an encouragement to single mothers. This is a bit of a testimony of my life. I could never tell it all. I had many trials and tribulations as a single mother, some because of disobedience. There were times when I would stop, put my hands up and say "Lord, why me?" When I look back and see, because of those trials, who God has allowed me to be and what He has allowed me to accomplish, I say "Why not me?"

I know what it is to be lied on, talked about, persecuted and thought of as unimportant or nobody. But I never did sit around and have a pity party (at least not long). I know what it is to do without in order for my children to have. I didn't do everything right and it wasn't an easy task, but one thing I did not neglect and that was bringing them up under the admonition of the Lord. Plant the seed while children are young and it will always be there; even though they may go astray sometimes when they grow older.

LET'S GET REAL

I say to the saved and unsaved single mothers, seek and continue to seek God and His righteousness and all other things will be added unto you. Don't seek the approval of man for that is a very costly mistake. Don't feel that you have to be a part of any clique or special group to feel good about yourself. God is all you need and He will give you who or whatever you need to make it and many of your desires.

Be a good mother. Discipline your children with love. Be there for them and they will be there for you; just as mine are here for me. Put your past behind and go on towards the mark for the prize of the high calling that Christ has for your life. He has forgiven your sins, now you must forgive yourself and others; then, go on walking in love (agape love). Sometimes we must learn to encourage ourselves and look to Jesus from where all our help comes. Keep your head up and be blessed above and beyond all of your expectation.

Let me share this with you. I went to nursing school and had children at home to manage. I came out on the honor roll every quarter. It wasn't easy but I had motivation and determination. God gave me strength, mentally and physically. God has a divine purpose for you and your children. They are not here by chance.

When I truly began to seek God, I was blessed above and beyond my highest expectation with a Godly husband whom I love very much. I love my children and they are very precious to me. I thank God for all who gave a helping hand in my accomplishments, even my enemies. All glory and honor goes to my Lord and Savior. So be encouraged! None of us have walked down the path of perfection. Love the Lord and no weapon formed against you will prosper. With God on your side you can and will make it. Let's get real!

www.ingramcontent.com/pod-product-compliance
Lightning Source LLC
Chambersburg PA
CBHW071714040426
42446CB00011B/2065